T0132256

THE UNEXPECTED
VISITOR

ANITA KHUTTAN

AuthorHouse™
1663 Liberty Drive
Bloomington, IN 47403
www.authorhouse.com
Phone: 1 (833) 262-8899

Because of the dynamic nature of the Internet, any web addresses or links contained in this book may have changed
since publication and may no longer be valid. The views expressed in this work are solely those of the author and do
not necessarily reflect the views of the publisher, and the publisher hereby disclaims any responsibility for them.

Any people depicted in stock imagery provided by Getty Images are models,
and such images are being used for illustrative purposes only.
Certain stock imagery © Getty Images.

This book is printed on acid-free paper.

Interior Image Credit: Anita Khuttan

ISBN: 978-1-6655-0484-3 (sc)
ISBN: 978-1-6655-0485-0 (e)

Library of Congress Control Number: 2020923481

Print information available on the last page.

Published by AuthorHouse 11/06/2020

authorHOUSE®

The Unexpected Visitor

Anita Khuttan

They did not even know of me at first.
No one really knows when I arrived.

I walked with them, sat and played,
no matter what their age or size.

I was lonely friends please understand. I did not know we'd multiply if we held hands.

Soon, there were more visitors like me. We were so happy together you see.

Then slowly my friends stopped coming to school. One with a cold, a cough, a sore throat, or something cruel.

I looked around and suddenly I figured,
I had made them poorly and so an idea
triggered.

Sadly, I unlocked my hands, and created a 2 metre distance.

I had to leave, you and me could not be in coexistence.

It's either them or either me...it was plain and simple I had to flee.

It was tough to leave, I took my time.
My reason was good enough to undo my crime.

I'll leave you with these special rules, to be safe and well, you need these tools...

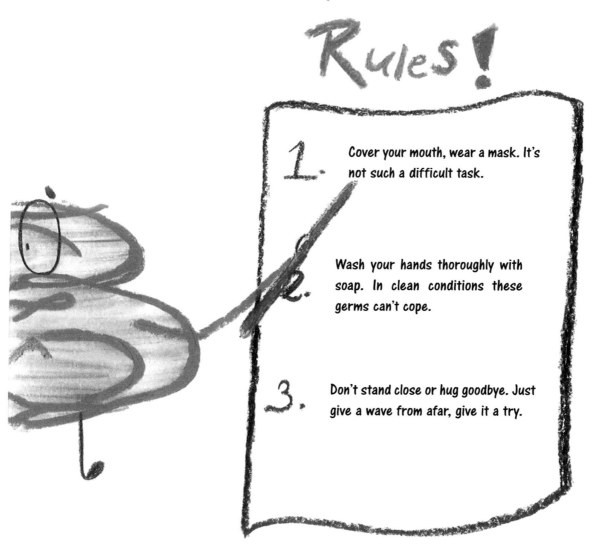

Rules!

1. Cover your mouth, wear a mask. It's not such a difficult task.

2. Wash your hands thoroughly with soap. In clean conditions these germs can't cope.

3. Don't stand close or hug goodbye. Just give a wave from afar, give it a try.

I was the Unexpected Visitor the world didn't want.

SORRY...

Printed in the United States
By Bookmasters